Scan Me.

MW01442827

Created with QRPics

In the enchanted forest, the Feathertons learned of love and compassion.

Mama Featherton shared, "Love others as God loves you, with kindness."

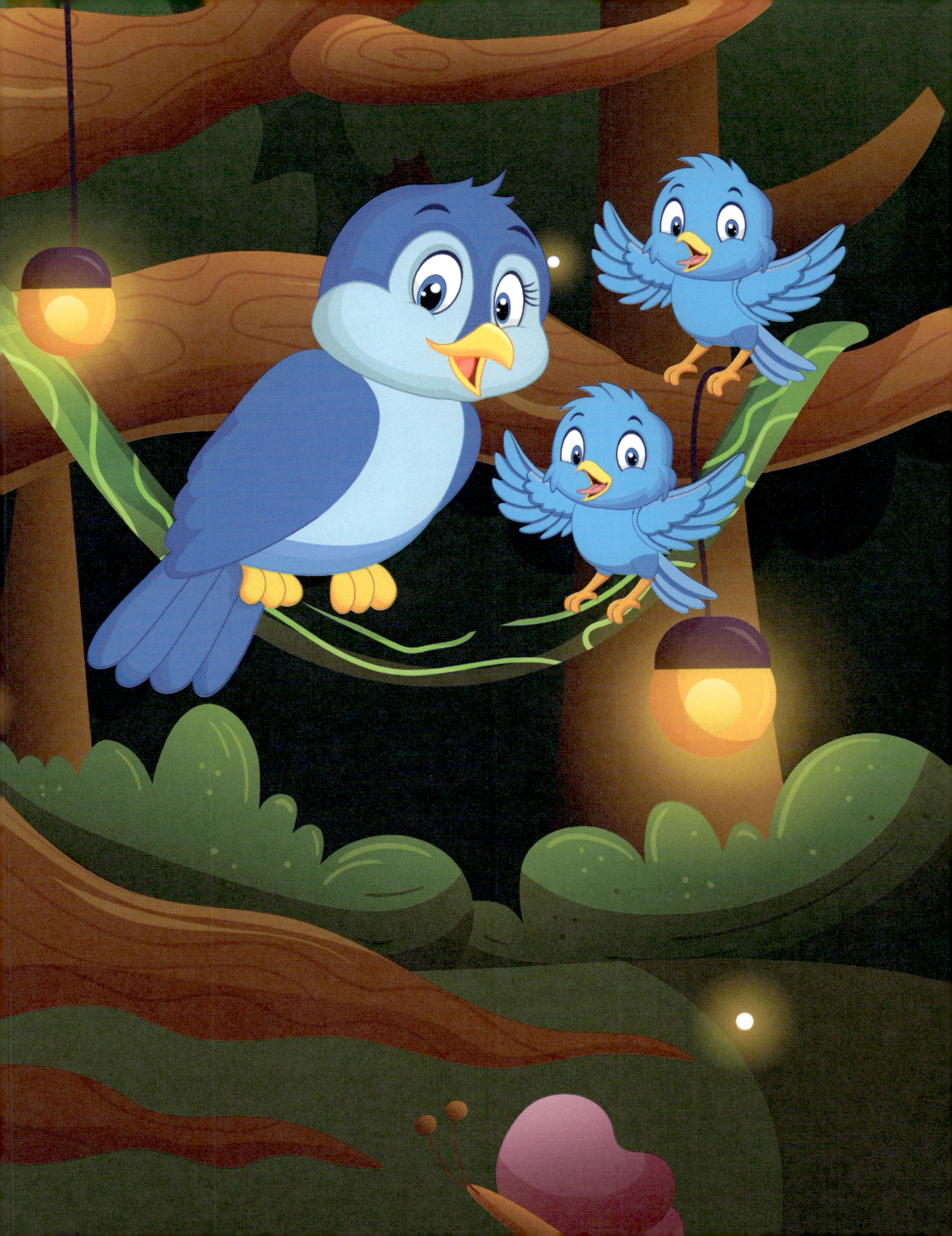

They met a lost bunny named Benny, shivering beneath a thicket.

Little Feather offered warmth, saying, "We'll be your forest family."